Left in the Shadows

MAPLE
PUBLISHERS

Left in the Shadows

Author: Frances Christie

Copyright © 2024 Frances Christie

The right of Frances Christie to be identified as the author of this work has been asserted by the author in accordance with section 77 and 78 of the Copyright, Designs and Patents Act 1988.

ISBN 978-1-83538-282-0 (Paperback)
978-1-83538-303-2 (Ebook)
978-1-83538-098-7 (Hardback)

Cover Design and Book Layout by:
White Magic Studios
www.whitemagicstudios.co.uk

Published by:
Maple Publishers
Fairbourne Drive, Atterbury,
Milton Keynes,
MK10 9RG, UK
www.maplepublishers.com

A CIP catalogue record for this title is available from the British Library.

All rights reserved. No part of this book may be reproduced or translated by any form or by any means, electronic or mechanical, including photocopying, recording or by any information storage and retrieval system without written permission from the author.

The views expressed in this work are solely those of the author and do not necessarily reflect the views of the publisher, and the publisher hereby disclaims any responsibility for them.

Unveiling forgotten histories one Shadow at a time

Preface

My research has been thorough, I have spent many hours pouring over various manuscripts, documents and newspaper articles. Everything I have written in this book is backed up by archived data revealing manipulation of facts and a deliberate attempt to hide the accomplishments made by people of African heritage.

I would sincerely like to thank my friend Geraldine Artuso who made valuable contributions to the finishing of this book.

Contents

Introduction	6
A Brief History	8
John Arrives in England	11
Polish entourage Relocates to Paris	16
A New Life for John is about to begin	21
Paris 1789	28
George takes London by Storm	34
John's Heritage	40
The Growth of England's Abolition Movement	50
John's contribution to the Cause	55
Haiti 1791	64
Secret Decree	77
John Polgreen Bridgetower	83
George Polgreen Bridgetower	87
Epilogue	102

Introduction

History often whispers the tales of exceptional individuals, their voices fading with time. This book looks into the fascinating times of the 18th and 19th centuries, drawing on a wealth of sources primarily newspaper articles, quotes and archived data. Within this timeline is the remarkable tale of John Polgreen Bridgetower, a man who defied the bonds of Jamaican slavery to carve a unique path among the upper echelons of European society.

Historiographers have swept John's significant achievements into obscurity, distorting some accounts, and leaving others lost in time, yet, through his own words and a thorough examination of the historical context, we can finally piece together the extraordinary journey of his life, a life that challenged all expectations, his freedom from slavery, his rise in European society, to his exile from England and his pivotal role as General Mentor to the Haitian revolutionary leader, Toussaint Louverture.

John's life stands as a testament to unwavering resilience. He not only secured his own freedom but paved the way for his son, George Bridgetower, a violin prodigy. George, from the age of six was already being recognised by musical giants such as Joseph Haydn, Ernst Schick, Chevalier de Saint-George.

Frankfurt Newspaper April 1786

George Bridgetower, son of a Moor and former valet to his most serene Royal Highness Prince Esterhazy. At seven years old he was pupil of the worthy Haydn, who had the favour of playing before his Majesty the Kaiser as well as in various princely courts to universal applause. We will have the honour, on Wednesday 5th April here in the concert room of the great Red House, to give a grand instrumental concert he will perform on the violin, in anticipation of warm encouragement from an honourable public starting precisely at 6 o'clock in the evening.

Beyond John's remarkable tale, lies the captivating, untold story of his son, George and his marriage to an English heiress, Mary Leake. Information taken from newspaper articles and archived data reveals Mary's scandalous affair with an Italian nobleman and her untimely demise, which cast a long shadow of suspicion.

A Brief History

Over twelve million people were taken from the Continent of Africa in order to enrich European countries, who were brutally colonising nations across the world. Several African kingdoms were involved in the first leg of the Transatlantic slave trade, the most affluent being the Kingdom of Dahomey (present day Benin). They raided villages in and around West Central Africa capturing men, women and children before taking them to trading ports known as the 'slave coast' There, European traders waited with ships laden with produce including guns, alcohol and textiles to exchange for innocent human lives.

The second leg, known as the Middle Passage, was a horrific journey for the captives, they were crammed onto ships like cattle and transported across the Atlantic to the Americas where they were sold like chattel mainly to plantation owners. They faced a brutal fate deemed acceptable by those who profited from their misery, blinded by greed, they viewed their human cargo as subhuman, unleashing unspeakable atrocities. The average lifespan of young men and women enslaved on a plantation was a mere seven years, a stark testimony to the barbarity they endured. The hidden cost of colonisation, the suffering of millions, remained unseen and unheard for centuries.

The final leg witnessed a grim transformation, ships that once carried stolen lives now returned to Europe loaded not with human cargo, but with the bitter fruits of forced labour, sugar, rum and other luxuries filled their holds, a grotesque bounty that masked the suffering that lined the pockets of European merchants. Several European nations were deeply implicated in the transatlantic slave trade, France, Portugal, England, Spain, Denmark, Sweden and the Netherlands all playing a significant role in this horrific enterprise.

Slave owners returning to Europe often brought their human property with them as a symbol of their wealth, this also included their own enslaved children brought to work as house servants, valets, maids and doormen. Others viewed slaves purely as commodities, to be sold or gifted, whilst a few offered a degree of familiarity, education and freedom. The vast majority endured a life defined by cruelty and exploitation.

In England alone, an estimated forty-six thousand slave owners profited handsomely from the slave trade. To perpetuate this system of exploitation they embarked on a cold-hearted mission, warping the minds of future generations. A web of lies was spun, portraying people with dark skin as inherently inferior, lacking both intellect and compassion. This insidious indoctrination served a purpose of ensuring enslaved people were worthy of the barbaric treatment inflicted upon them.

The 1810 Encyclopaedia Britannic

> Negro, 'as this unhappy race are strangers to every sentiment of compassion and an awful example of the corruption of man left to himself.

The vile attempt to brand Africans as inherently inferior could not extinguish their brilliance. Instead, many rose above oppression, defying expectations and thriving in a multitude of fields, inventors, writers, poets, musicians, soldiers and explorers; an indication of their boundless human spirit.

However, this growing African excellence posed a direct threat to the established order, by the early 1800s, a chilling response emerged from the ruling classes, a systematic erasure campaign was launched, aiming to purge any African presence from positions of respect or admiration on every platform of European society. This assault was not just about controlling the present; it was a deliberate attempt to crush any aspirations for future generations.

Part 1

John Arrives in England

British newspapers in 1767 were filled with reports of a brewing conflict between Russia and Poland; a large, royal entrouge had arrived in England from Poland. With them was eight-year-old Prince Hieronim Radziwill, heir to one of Europe's wealthiest dynasties. He was in the care of his uncle and was to remain in exile until the situation in his homeland subsided. At the same time a transatlantic slave ship returned to England from Barbados. Thirteen-year-old John Polgreen, an enslaved boy, disembarked from the ship; destined to be sold or gifted away.

Leeds Intelligencer Newspaper 28 July 1767

> *A body of Russian troops, with a large artillery, is cantoned around the place, in order to preserve the public tranquillity and order and protect the deputies of the confederacy. Two of those belonging to Lithuania arrived here within a few days, one of whom is a young Prince Radziwill.*

Though Poland was not a participant in the slave trade, John, became a personal valet for Prince Radziwill. This unlikely encounter released him from slavery and altered the course of his life.

Eighteenth century England began to witness a seismic shift. The long held beliefs that Africans were devoid of intellect and compassion began to crumble under the weight of reality. An estimated twenty thousand Africans living within the country itself served as a living challenge to these ingrained prejudices, their presence fostered a promising questioning of the very legality of slavery.

A young boy named Jonathan Strong was also headline news in 1767. He had been brought to England from Barbados two years earlier. His enslaver was a man of despicable character, he planned to ship Jonathan back to the horrors of the colonies. Knowing all too well of the barbarity there, Jonathan made a desperate bid for freedom and ran away. His escape was short lived; slave catchers snatched him from the streets of London and returned him to his tormentor, who in a fit of rage beat Jonathan, leaving him barely clinging to life, he then threw him into the street like unwanted refuse.

Unknown to his enslaver, help came to Jonathan in the form of William Sharp, a London doctor famed for his charitable work of treating the poor.

Doctor Sharp's brother, Granville Sharp, was a British scholar and humanitarian; they both were deeply upset by Jonathan's gruesome injuries. They compassionately shouldered the burden of his four month stay at London's St Bartholomew's Hospital. Whilst the treatment helped him recover, it could not erase the lasting damage to his body.

A Memorial Plaque at St Bartholomew's Hospital

William and Granville's kindness went beyond; they secured a job for Jonathan with a Quaker friend of theirs. However, his newfound freedom proved fragile. When his former enslaver spotted him, he recaptured and imprisoned Jonathan, claiming absolute ownership of him and his right to sell him at will.

When word of his capture got to Granville Sharp it ignited a fire within him. Determined to secure his freedom, he wasted no time, he demanded a hearing before the Lord Mayor and assembled a team of skilled lawyers to defend Jonathan in court.

Granville Sharp

1735 – 1813

In a landmark decision in 1767 the Lord Mayor ruled that Jonathan's capture and threatened deportation were unlawful as he had committed no crime. He was therefore freed from slavery; he was nineteen years old.

Although this was a victory for individual freedom it did not abolish slavery itself, it did however set a precedent for the future. For Granville Sharp, his encounter with Jonathan Strong was the very beginning of a lifelong campaign to dismantle the barbaric institution of slavery in the British Empire.

Jonathan Strong's freedom was short-lived; his body succumbed to the injuries inflicted by his tormentor.

Granville Sharps wrote in his diary 19 April 1773

(Gloucestershire Archives B3549 13/4/2)

Poor Jonathan Strong, the first Negro whose freedom I had procured in 1767, died this morning.

Jonathan Strong

1747 - 1773

Eighty years after Jonathan Strong's passing an image emerged from Liverpool. This painting was not just a portrait of a young boy, it served as a poignant reminder of the thousands of young men and women who were brought and enslaved in England.

Jonathan's plight simply brought awareness to the streets of London for the first time, as many people witnessed the sheer brutality enslaved people had to endure.

Part 2

Polish Entourage Relocates to Paris

Three years in London had transformed John under the prince's instruction. He mastered the Polish language and customs and took Bridgetower as his surname.

The conflict in Poland remained unresolved, with Polish nobles and gentry continuing to fight to safeguard their country's independence from Russian influence. As a result, the young prince and his entourage were still unable to return home.

Their next destination was France which was abuzz with preparations for a lavish royal wedding; fifteen year old Louis Augustus Dauphin of France was to wed fourteen-year-old Austrian Princess Marie Antoinette. Amid the whirlwind of pageantry, a new chapter in John's life began to unfold, as he encountered Chevalier de Saint-Georges, a man of mixed heritage, whose very existence embodied the era's many contradictions.

Chevalier's father was a French aristocrat with close ties to the king. He had travelled to Guadeloupe, a French colony in the West Indies years earlier, whilst there he purchased a beautiful, enslaved woman of sixteen years old, Chevalier's mother. When he was still a young child his father brought them to live in France as a family.

In France Chevalier thrived, his undeniable talent blossoming on a stage built of paradox. His lineage bore privilege and oppression, the son of both aristocracy and enslavement. By the age of twenty four Chevalier had become a public phenomenon in France, admired and respected by all, he excelled as a virtuoso violinist, composer, athlete and swordsman. He navigated the world of French courtiers with ease, his education impeccable and his reputation for brilliance established.

Chevalier de Saint George

1745-1799.

As preparations for the royal wedding reached a fever pitch, Europe's most celebrated musicians received invitations to perform at the wedding. Chevalier's contributions to French classical music all but assured his involvement in the music for the royal wedding.

Despite his public acclaim and noble bearing. French law denied Chevalier the legal right to his title or marriage due to his African heritage.

The royal wedding took place at the beautiful Palace of Versailles on 16th May 1770. Marie Antoinette wore a magnificent lilac gown, adorned with diamonds and pearls, Prince Louis wore an outfit of silver. A crowd of two hundred thousand waited outside the palace for a glimpse of the royal couple. For fifteen days festivities consumed Versailles. Extravagant meals, dazzling performances and glittering balls to mark the occasion. The grand finale was a spectacular firework display that promised.to illuminate the night sky.

Thousands of Parisians packed the streets to get a glimpse of the fireworks. Disaster struck when the wooden structure upon which the fireworks were launched caught fire. Panic ripped through the crowd, triggering a stampede that left hundreds dead and thousands injured. Prince Louis and Marie Antoinette were distraught to hear about the tragic accident.

They offered their condolences and donated their personal allowance for a month to the victims' families. However, this gesture did little to quell the rising tide of anger. The horrific accident served as a reminder of the vast gulf separating the opulent lives of the aristocracy from the daily struggles of the common people. Words of discontent echoed around the city. The lavish display of wealth, coupled with the tax breaks enjoyed by the upper classes contrasted sharply with the harsh realities faced by the poor, who could barely afford to feed their families. The incident added to the growing resentment towards the monarchy.

France proved a fertile ground for John. Immersed in the Polish entourage, he readily absorbed the French language and customs. But his education extended far beyond the classroom.

The presence of Chevalier de Saint-Georges, a man of exceptional musical talent and charisma, cast a spell on John. He devoured every performance, inspiring his own possibilities. Chevalier's influence would become a defining force in John's future.

Two years into their Parisian stay, news from across the Channel swirled with a confusing mix of hope and uncertainty. A new law had been passed in England, one that many interpreted as the end of slavery throughout the British Empire.

In a landmark case in London. James Somerset, a young man, enslaved and taken to England from Jamaica; he too absconded when his owner planned to return him to the colonies. He was brutally recaptured and chained on a slave ship. His plight reached the ears of abolitionists; who were determined to fight for his freedom.

They took his case to court Somerset v Stewart. Presiding over the case was Chief Justice William Murray, 1st Earl of Mansfield. After a complex argument on the legality of chattel slavery in England, William Murray delivered a pivotal ruling. He declared that slavery was not supported by English law whilst on English soil; enslaved people were to be considered servants not property and could not be returned to the colonies against their will.

Quote by William Murry

> *The air of England is too pure for a slave to breath, and so everyone who breathes it becomes free. Everyone who comes to this island is entitled to the protection of English law, whatever oppression he may have suffered and whatever may be the colour of his skin.*

The Somerset verdict proved a limited victory, outraged slave owners across the British Empire ignored the ruling, returning their "property" to the colonies whenever they desired. The law's reach, unfortunately, extended only as far as the willingness of the powerful to enforce it, for the enslaved freedom remained a precarious hope.

Part 3

A New Life for John Was About to Begin

The Polish-Russian conflict ended in 1772 leaving behind a peace settlement. Russia emerged triumphant, initiating the first of several partitions of Poland. After five years in exile, the young Prince Radziwill, now thirteen years old, could finally return home to Biala Podlaska.

Under Prince Radziwill's patronage, John blossomed into a young man of eighteen. As the prince's personal valet he was always by his side, enabling John to fully embrace Polish culture. His exceptional linguistic talents flourished, remarkably fluent in five languages: Polish, English, French, Italian, and German. He was well known and sought-after as a translator among the aristocracy; John's fluency solidified his position as a vital asset within the magnificent Radziwill dynasty.

In the royal game of alliances marriages between princes and princesses served as a powerful tool to secure peace between nations, such was that of Sophie Friederike, a young German Princess from the House of Thurn and Taxis, betrothed since childhood to Prince Radziwill.

On her sixteenth birthday she embarked on a journey to Poland, accompanied by a grand entourage, where a lavish royal wedding awaited her; their wedding took place on 31st December 1775.

Prince Radziwill   **Princess Sophia**

A spark ignited between John and Maria Schmidt, one of Princess Sophia's German companions. With the blessing of Prince Radziwill and Princess Sophia, their love blossomed into marriage.

Before the wedding ceremony John underwent a baptism, taking the name Friederike, a gesture perhaps acknowledging his new German family, he would be known as John Polgreen Friederike Bridgetower.

On a joyous 11th October 1778 John and Maria welcomed a son into the world, the baby was named George Polgreen Bridgetower, perhaps bearing a silent tribute to Chevalier de Saint-Georges, the celebrated violinist John had admired in France.

Eleven years by Prince Radziwill's side had forged a deep bond between them, hence he and Princess Sophia became George's godparents, many military leaders and aristocracy attended the baptism. His baptism names were Hieronymus Hyppolitus de Augustus.

Two years after George's arrival another son, Friederike, joined the family. John, however, couldn't shake the angst for their future; their African heritage, a source of pride for him, could become a dangerous burden for his sons in this world. He vowed in a heartfelt letter, a promise etched in ink, that slavery would never be their fate. John took a proactive approach, personally overseeing their education, etiquette, music and the languages he himself had mastered. These were the tools he equipped them with, determined to carve a path for his sons to thrive in a world stacked against them.

Music lessons revealed hidden talents in both boys, but George possessed a talent that went beyond aptitude, he mastered the violin, his fingers dancing across the strings with a grace that mirrored John's idol, Chevalier de Saint-Georges. A growing sense of awe tinged with a hint of fear, as he watched his son, this wasn't just talent; it was genius. In George he saw the potential for a future unlike any he could have imagined, a future where music could transcend societal boundaries.

John's own versatile talents, his linguistic fluency, artistic knowledge and familiarity with European culture opened a door for the family. Prince Nikolaus II Esterházy, a titan among Austro-Hungarian nobility, extended a desirable position for John. The prince, a renowned patron of the arts, held court in a palace that housed not only a grand opera house but also a private orchestra led by the legendary Franz Joseph Haydn.

Joseph Haydn

1732-1809

Joseph Haydn had been the musical director of the Esterhazy court for some eighteen years, he wasn't just a prolific composer in the world of classical music, his output was monumental, wielding the baton as the Prince's Kapellmeister, his passion, dedication and brilliance resonated far beyond the palace walls, securing him a place as one of Europe's most celebrated composers.

John, ever the strategist, saw Esterházy's offer as a launchpad for his sons' futures He uprooted his family and moved to Austria taking a position as Prince Esterházy's personal valet. Beyond his duties John became an unofficial palace ambassador. His multilingual skills and cultural expertise made him the perfect guide for aristocratic visitors. He delighted them with tours, showcasing the breathtaking architecture, exquisite paintings and of course the magnificent concert halls.

Esterhazy Palace

Meanwhile, John's pride swelled as he witnessed George's talent explode under the instruction of Joseph Haydn. Young George was no longer just learning; he was flourishing. The strings of his violin serenaded not just the Esterházy court but also the esteemed European gentry and royalty who graced the palace.

Despite the prestigious environment, a concern gnawed at John, the Esterházy palace's rural isolation could stifle George's burgeoning talent. John was a well connected gentleman, he promoted his son and secured concert opportunities across Europe, propelling them out of the palace and into the wider musical landscape. Germany beckoned as their next destination, their arrival in Germany was a triumph. George's virtuosity cast a spell, captivating audiences whose admiration was effusive.

Frankfurt Newspaper April 1786

> *George Bridgetower, son of a moor and former valet to his most serene Prince Esterhazy, seven years old, a pupil of the worthy Haydn, who had the favour of playing before his Majesty the Kaiser. As well as in various Princely courts to universal applause, will have the honour on Wednesday 5th April here in the concert room of the great Red House, to give a grand instrumental concert in which he will perform on the violin, in anticipation of warm encouragement from an honourable public. starting at precisely at 6 o'clock in the evening*

A dark shadow fell upon John and Maria's growing family with the tragic loss of their third son, Johannes Albertus, in infancy. During this sombre period they met with Ernst Schick, a virtuoso violinist, he instantly recognized young George's talent. Together, a musical partnership blossomed, their combined talents soon graced concert stages across Germany, culminating in a performance for Joseph II, the Holy Roman Emperor of the Habsburg Empire and brother of Marie Antoinette.

George was a rising star; his genius was so mesmerising that concert offers poured in from all over Europe. In March of 1789 his brilliance shone on two grand stages. First, he performed for the Dutch Prince William V of Orange, by prestigious command. Next, he took centre stage for a public concert in the Hague, Netherlands. The appreciative audience was left awestruck by his performance, their thunderous applause an indication of his brilliance.

Opportunities arose with invitations to perform in both France and England. France beckoned first with a prestigious commission to perform a violin concerto by the Italian virtuoso, Giovanni Battista. Knowing the significance of this moment John and Marie decided he would take George to France then England, while she stayed in Germany to care for their younger son Friederike.

Neither John nor Maria knew it would be the last time they would see each other and the last time John would see his young son Friederike.

Part 4

Paris 1789

Seventeen years had transformed France into a nation John barely recognized. Memories of the grand royal wedding, now a distant echo tarnished by the fireworks disaster lingered in some Parisian minds. But these faded memories paled compared to the inferno gripping the social landscape. France teetered on the brink of revolution, decades of unchecked inequality had carved a chasm between the extravagant lives of the elite and the desperate plight of the poor. Years of failed harvests sent bread prices skyrocketing, an irony in a land known for its abundance, the government's suffocating weight of taxation further burdened a populace already on the verge of starvation.

This was the Age of Enlightenment, a time when reason challenged tradition. The impoverished questioned not only their dire circumstances, but the very system that perpetuated them. The once-genteel street of Paris now crackled with palpable tension, an indication of the coming storm. Dread washed over the ruling classes throughout the nation.

Whilst still adored by Parisian audiences, Chevalier de Saint-Georges embarked on a mission: to establish a French chapter of the anti-slavery movement.

Mirroring the efforts of Thomas Clarkson and Granville Sharp, who had begun the abolition fight across the English Channel two years prior. He worked with passionate figures like Jacques Pierre Brissot and Maximilien Robespierre, their revolutionary ideals resonating deeply with his own sense of justice.

"The Society of the Friends of the Blacks" was a boldly defiant name, a strong call that directly challenged the very system powering French colonial wealth. These men and women, hailing from vastly different backgrounds, were bound by a shared belief in liberty and equality. Their vision, however, extended far beyond the abolition of slavery, foreshadowing the radical upheaval that would soon engulf France.

On the 13th April 1789 anticipation rang through the Concert Spiritual Hall. The young virtuoso, George Bridgetower, was to perform. Among the distinguished audience sat Thomas Jefferson, the American minister to France and himself a fellow violinist. Gloating from the American Revolution's triumph over Britain, Jefferson carried a keen interest in the expanding revolutionary spirit simmering beneath the surface of French society.

Jefferson's daughter, Martha, accompanied him in Paris, alongside Sally Hemings, a young woman enslaved by the Jefferson family. Sally was half-sister to Martha's deceased mother, despite their family connection.

Sally remained enslaved as Jefferson maintained the belief that people with dark skin were intellectually and creatively inferior to people with white skin, justifying the system of human bondage.

Sally Hemings

1773-1835

Thomas Jefferson

1743-1826

Jefferson was forty-six years old at this time: his views on race simply by passed his daughter's personal slave. Sally, who was just sixteen years old. With little choice, was already carrying the first of six children that he had with her, four of whom survived into adulthood.

He freed his children from slavery before he died. But Sally remained his property, kept in bondage, even after his death. The hypocrisy of Jefferson, who championed liberty whilst denying it to those closest to him.

Eleven years after he left France, Thomas Jefferson became the President of the United States. The man who penned the now iconic words, "all men are created equal," in the Declaration of Independence, held a deeply conflicted stance on slavery.

Despite his revolutionary rhetoric, Jefferson remained a slaveholder himself. The economic benefits of slavery were undeniable and the institution itself was deeply entrenched in southern society. While Jefferson may have recognized the hypocrisy of his position, he lacked the political will or courage to dismantle the system.

The noble ideals enshrined in the American Declaration of Independence couldn't escape the scrutiny of brilliant minds like Benjamin Banneker, an African American mathematician and astronomer. In a bold move, Banneker wrote a letter to Jefferson, highlighting the hypocrisy of a nation declaring freedom while still clinging to the institution of slavery.

The Declaration of Independence

> *"We hold these truths to be self-evident, that all men are created equal, that they are endowed by their Creator with certain unalienable Rights that among these are Life, Liberty and the pursuit of Happiness".*

Jefferson's response to Banneker's charged letter was a masterclass in deflection. He readily condemned slavery in the abstract, calling it a "moral depravity and a hideous blot." However, a lofty rhetoric rang hollow considering his own extensive ownership of slaves.

While commending Banneker on his achievements, a patronising undertone was evident. Jefferson diminished Banneker's individual brilliance and reinforced ethnic stereotypes, describing him as a credit to the black race.

Benjamin Banneker

1731-1818

Ironically Jefferson, who harboured such biased beliefs, was attending a concert in Paris to witness a ten-year-old prodigy, a black violinist whose talent went beyond categorization, he was accompanied by his father, John Bridgetower, whose sharp eyes scanned the prestigious Parisian Hall. Taking in every detail, his posture ramrod straight as he and his son proudly displayed black excellence and intellect. This was a silent statement in a fight for the injustice bestowed on African people. Breaking down the delusional beliefs held by Europeans about black inferiority.

A fascinating performance unfolded that night as George Bridgetower stood centre stage, his violin weaving a tapestry of melody with a concerto by the famed Italian composer, Giovanni Giornovichi. George did not disappoint, as the final notes faded, a hush fell over the concert hall, then, a thunderous eruption of applause; the audience amazed by the talent of the young boy. French newspapers raved about his performance.

Le Mercure de France: April 1789

"His talent is one of the best replies one can give to philosophers who wish to deprive people of his nation and his colour of the opportunity to distinguish themselves in the arts.

Although reviews for George's performance were glowing, France was on the brink, just three weeks after his performance riots erupted on the streets of Paris; led by Maximilien Robespierre. The once grand boulevards of Paris became a battleground; thousands of French nationals, mainly from the upper classes were leaving France at an alarming rate, it was becoming increasingly unsafe for them to remain.

Part 5

George Takes London by Storm

John had accepted a prestigious invitation from HRH the Prince of Wales, who had invitied them to stay at the newly built Brighton Pavilion. He also sponsored George whilst he was in England.

Chester Chronicle 14th August 1789:

> *The musical world is likely to be enriched by the greatest phenomenon ever heard. A youth of ten years old, pupil of the immortal Haydn he performs the most difficult pieces on the violin and goes through all the mazes of sound with wonderful spirit, execution and delicacy. His name is Bridgetower, a stable plant of an African growth: Thus, do we find that genius does not solely belong to the tincture of the skin." He is now at Brighton Pavilion, under the patronage of the prince of Wales".*

Their arrival in England was met with excitement, as the news of a phenomenal child prodigy had preceded them, many people were eager to see this boy first-hand. Newspaper reporters, with their pens poised, awaited the chance to chronicle the brilliance of the young violinist.

London Chronicle Sept 1789:

"A young Negro named George Bridgetower, has made his entre into the world as a musician and promises to be one of the first players in Europe. His natural genius was first cultivated by the celebrated Haydn: he speaks many languages"

Young George Bridgetower

1778- 1860

Portrait by Henry Edridge 1790

A shadow of despair hungover the British royal court, King George III, was deeply affected by the loss of thirteen colonies in the American Revolution, he had descended into a debilitating depression.

In an attempt to lift the king's spirits, the Prince of Wales held a private concert to cheer up the King and Queen in a time of national and personal grief.

The Prince of Wales was a vain reckless young man, He squandered vast sums of public funds on lavish soirees, gambling sprees, and endless rounds of fine liquor. When the government dared to raise an eyebrow at this extravagance, the prince, with an arrogant dismissal, clung to the delusion of his own limitless wealth. His mounting debts, however, became a national concern, the House of Commons, in a desperate bid to avert financial disaster was forced to increase his income and pay off his debts.

HRH The Prince of Wales

1762 - 1830

Undeterred by criticism, the prince embarked on the creation of a pleasure palace: the Brighton Pavilion. This extravagant seaside retreat, a secluded sanctuary unlike any other rose with domes and towers. Within its opulent walls lavish entertainment unfolded for his chosen companions, serenaded by his own orchestra. Here, away from the watchful eyes of both the public and the government, the prince could indulge his every whim. The prince's opponents were outraged at the build of the Royal Pavilion, they saw this as an abuse of power, a waste of public funds and a social injustice.

This was a period in England when orphans roamed the streets and huddled in doorways for shelter, thousands of infants perished each year; the victims of malnutrition and filthy water. Little compassion came from the upper classes. They blamed the poor's suffering on their own shortcomings: ignorance, laziness, and vice. This attitude ensured there would be little relief for the most desperate members of society.

A Street in the Slums

The last resort for the poor was the dreaded workhouses, a breeding ground for despair. Sickness and disease ran rampant caused by overcrowding and neglect. Children were separated from their parents and forced into harsh labour, men, women, and the elderly toiled endlessly. Some ninety thousand destitute people endured a brutal existence in the unforgiving walls of the workhouse. Designed to be a deterrent, to discourage the poor from seeking help from government funds.

On 25th September 1789 George and his father arrived at Queen Charlotte's private Lodge in Windsor Castle. George took to the stage, his bow drawing bright melodies as he played a violin concerto by composer Viotti and a quartet by the composer Joseph Haydn, the royal audience was entranced by the young virtuoso's talent.

Windsor Castle

By the tender age of ten George had already played before many royal courts across Europe. He delivered a performance that left everyone breathless, his poised demeanour and virtuosic skill on the violin were a masterclass in musicality, even the Prince of Wales, a notoriously discerning patron of the arts, found himself speechless with admiration, As the final notes faded. The prince saw a precious jewel this young prodigy.

Mrs Charlotte Papendiek was Assistant Keeper of the Wardrobe for Queen Charlotte, who had recorded the occasion in her diary.

> *"An adventurer by the name Bridgetower, a black, came to Windsor with the view of introducing his son, a most possessing lad of ten or twelve years old, an excellent violin player. He was commanded by their Majesties to perform at the Lodge [the Queen's Lodge], where he played a concerto of Viotti's and a quartet of Haydn's whose pupil he called himself. Both father and son pleased greatly, the son for his talent and modest bearing, the father for his fascinating manner, elegance, expertness in all languages, beauty of a person, and taste in dress,* "He seemed to win the opinion of everyone and was courted by all."

British news reporters descended upon John, eager to hear about his own remarkable story. Seizing the opportunity, he recounted the history of his father the Abyssinian Prince, his intention, simply to identify the injustice of slavery.

Part 6

John's Heritage

The Solomonic dynasty ruled the Kingdom of Abyssinia, present day Ethiopia and Eritrea. From the 13th century it was one of the longest surviving empires in history and claimed direct descent from the biblical King Solomon and the Queen of Sheba.

Abyssinian Crest

Abyssinia's allure for Europeans was complicated. Its unwavering Christian faith, evident in an abundance of churches, monasteries and castles, that stood as beacons in the country. Their strong faith, however, proved a double-edged sword. Whilst it helped Abyssinia resist formal colonisation, it could not fully deflect European greed. the gold, diamonds and ancient artefacts belonging to the Empire became a siren song for European fortune seekers. Their materialism was a constant threat to Abyssinia's sovereignty.

The Fasil Ghebbi fortress was built in the seventeenth century by Emperor Fasilides, it was one of the royal residences of the Abyssinian rulers.

Fasil Ghebbi

In the early eighteenth century, a Dutch sea captain on an expedition to Abyssinia was entrusted with a mission of immense importance. He was to transport a young, educated prince, destined to learn the intricacies of European law and customs. Lavished with a treasure trove of gold and diamonds as payment, the captain set sail, but treachery lurked beneath his façade, not long after they set sail, the tides turned.

The supposed guardian transformed into a monstrous captor, brutally mistreating the prince and stealing his wealth, with an unsympathetic heart, sold him like chattel into the cruel grip of slavery. He was bought by a British plantation owner and taken to Jamaica.

His enslaver, perhaps struck by the prince's distinct east African features, Christian heritage and his evident education, assigned him to serve within the grand house. Even permitted him to take a wife, a woman born native to Jamaica, their marriage, a mockery of their union, as it held no legal weight. European law considered them chattel (property), denying them any form of human or civil rights.

In 1754 the prince and his wife welcomed a son, born into the brutal reality of slavery, he was named John, within him he carried the untouchable birthright of an Abyssinian Prince, a direct descendant of King Solomon and the Queen of Sheba, a proud heritage that would live within him forever.

Haunted by the oppressors' intent to erase their past, the prince knew he had a sacred duty. Forbidden to speak their native tongues, to share stories of their families nor to practise the traditions of their ancestors, the enslaved community faced a relentless assault on their identity.

The prince, fired by a strong determination, sought a secret path. He told the story of their ancestry under the cloak of night whispering of a bygone Africa, of a lineage stretching back hundreds of years. In these stolen moments he planted the seed of his heritage within his son, John, a seed that would defy the oppressors' vile attempts to extinguish their past.

Jamaica

When John was six years old the British authorities implemented the 'divide-and-conquer' strategy to stop slaves from forming family units or friendships on the plantations. Those that had been formed were torn apart by splitting families or friendships, sending them to different plantations or colonies; this came about because of a revolt that took place in Jamaica on Easter Sunday 1760.

The revolt was led by Tacky, a warrior-king ripped from his homeland. The rebellion roared to life, overpowering British forces, they seized firearms and gunpowder. The fuel for freedom swept across Jamaica, flames destroying plantations, symbols of their harsh existence and the source of their oppressor's wealth. Every plantation torched became a ray of hope, inspiring more enslaved men and women to join the growing, formidable resistance.

Facing an expanding rebellion, Jamaica's Governor frantically petitioned King George III for extra reinforcements to suppress the slaves, also calling on the Jamaican Maroons, the descendants of runaway slaves, who had carved out a fragile freedom two decades before. They signed a treaty with the British Empire, who offered them an uneasy independence, it separated them from the enslaved population, but they were still bound to the colonial system.

The Maroons could not harbour runaway slaves; instead they would have to help capture them, a vicious alliance, knowing the Maroons would crush the rebellion to preserve their own precarious peace.

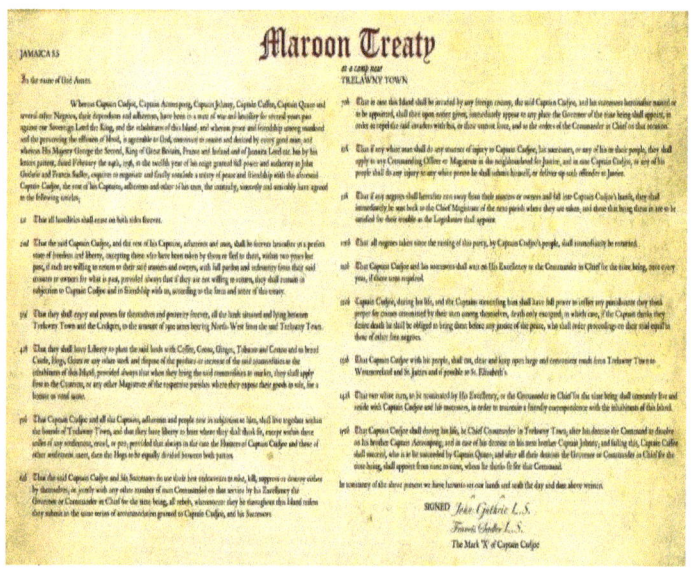

This tactic caused a split between the Maroons and the rest of the Jamaican population, dividing the country so slaves could not band together and draw on their own strength, after several months the leaders of the revolt were hunted down by the Maroons, who shot Tacky and several hundred rebels. Those that had been captured, were swiftly handed over to the British authorities who publicly tortured, then executed them to discourage more uprising.

Nonetheless, news of Tacky's rebellion spread across Jamaica, inspiring even more uprisings. Although British colonialists celebrated victory time and time again the unrest in the country caused many slave owners to flee Jamaica, leaving their overseers to run their plantations which led to even more unspeakable brutality and more rebellions.

Remembrance Plaque

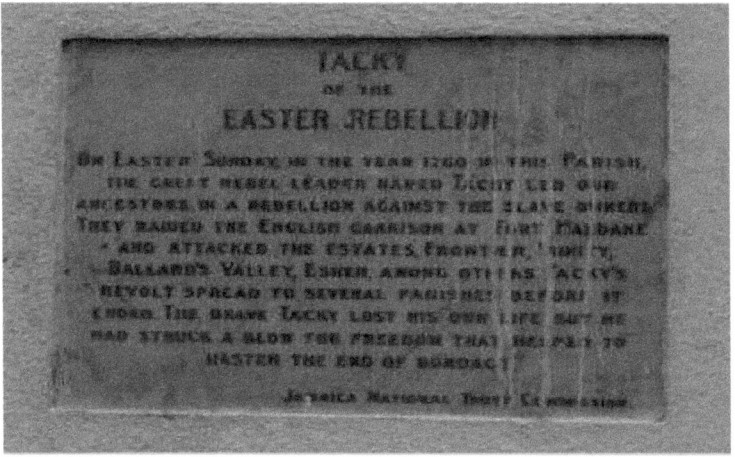

The relentless fires that consumed Jamaican plantations wasn't just a symbol of resistance, it was a blow to the very foundation of the British Empire. These persistent rebellions across the west Indian colonies weren't mere inconveniences; they were a powerful force chipping away at the economic justification of slavery, ultimately becoming a major catalyst for its eradication.

Polgreen Hotel Barbados

The rebellion's aftermath separated John from his parents, he wasn't sent to another plantation he was fortunate to be shipped to Bridgetown, Barbados and thrust into the sphere of James Polgreen's prestigious hotel this establishment catered to a glittering clientele of gentlemen, British naval officers and even royalty. Slaves were groomed into a different kind of servitude; trained to the high standards of gentlemen's valets, doormen, maids, and cooks. John, caught in this whirlwind of transition, received the name Polgreen and embarked on a new path as a valet.

Rachel Lauder was a young girl who frequented the magnificent Polgreen Hotel, it was her refuge. Escaping the odious character of her enslaver, a man who bore the sickening title of her "Father" William Lauder. A Scottish schoolmaster, who left Scotland for the warmer climate of the West Indies, her mother was a young Barbadian woman whom he bought, he subjected her and their young daughter Rachel to unimaginable cruelty.

Rachel's father eventually sold her to Captain Thomas Pringle of HMS Ariadne; he was charmed by her beauty and spirit. Before he left Barbados he freed her from the shackles of slavery and bought the Polgreen hotel for her along with nineteen people already enslaved there.

The hotel flourished, among her many patrons was Prince William, a frequent visitor; he was a young man on a fast track to the English throne. Known for his carefree revelry and impulsive behaviour, he'd earned the unflattering nickname "Silly Billy" from his peers.

One fateful night, drink and boisterous company, the prince's carelessness took a destructive turn. In a senseless rampage, he left a trail of ruin in his wake. Rachel's meticulously maintained hotel bearing the brunt of his royal tantrum.

Prince William 1V

1765-1837

The morning after, the wreckage was revealed. Rachel, not intimidated by HRH, presented him with a bill for the damages. Respectfully he paid enough, not just for the repairs, but elevating the hotel to even grander heights.

Rachel's refurbished establishment continued its tradition of impeccable service for gentlemen. Beautiful, Barbadian women selected by Rachel became part of the discrete appeal of the hotel. This was a time when there was no law against the sexual abuse of enslaved men women or children, this establishment was unique and protected.

Rachel Pringle Polgreen

By Thomas Rowlandson, London.
1753-1791

Far from reality, this portrait of Rachel Pringle Polgreen is a caricature, a skewed image crafted by a satirist five years after her death. When Rachel died the hotel was taken over by another freed Barbadian woman and ran successfully for another thirty years, until it burned down in 1821.

After newspaper reports went out about John he was dubbed the "African Prince" his heritage unveiled a tantalising glimpse into his background and ancestry, a rare, traceable thread that led back to Africa, a stark contrast to a life otherwise defined by slavery.

At a concert held in Bath during the autumn season of 1789, Hester Lynch Thrale Piozzi, wife of the musician Gabriele Mario Piozzi, documented a greater interest in John, surpassing the evening's celebrated prodigy.

> *Little Bridgetower. A boy not quite ten years old plays on the violin like a 1st rate performer and as the best proof of merit, is paid like one, Bridgetower is a Mulatto, son of a polish Duchess we are told and to an African Negro, the handsomest of his kind and colour ever seen, the father is with him, he wears an Eastern Habit and has an address so peculiarly, so singularly fine, no words will easily describe it, lofty politeness and vivacious hilarity were never so combined in any human creature that I have hitherto met with, splendid acquirements to, with an astonishing skill in languages and such power of conversation as can scarce be destroyed by his own rage of displaying it adorn the manners of the father, who were he less wonderful would please better.*

Whilst Hester offers a glimpse of John's personality, acknowledging his astonishing skills in languages, his politness and skillful conversation, however there's some awkwardness in her note, "adorn the manners of the father, who were he less wonderful would please better".

Part 7

The Growth of England's Abolition Movement

Whilst George's musical talent continued to enthral audiences, John joined the anti-slavery movement, a cause championed by the Quakers and led by the influential Anglican clergyman, Thomas Clarkson, the 18th century's most prominent anti-slavery campaigner in the British Empire, Clarkson becoming a lifelong advocate for the freedom of British slaves.

Thomas Clarkson

1760-1846

Sparking the flames of the anti-slavery movement, Thomas Clarkson and Granville Sharp joined forces to establish the Committee for the Abolition of the Slave Trade, they attracted a growing constellation of influential figures, including William Murray, James Ramsay, William Wilberforce, William Sharp, James Stevens, Hannah More, James Eliot, Zachary Macaulay, Henry Thornton and many more.

Despite their intense commitment and their impressive education, these abolitionists initially faced an uphill battle, struggling to gain traction for their cause.

William Wilberforce

1759-1833

In a groundbreaking moment in British history, William Wilberforce, the revered Member of Parliament and philanthropist, took the floor on 12th May 1789. For three hours, he held Parliament spellbound, his voice laden with the harrowing accounts written by Thomas Clarkson. Wilberforce painted the full picture of the barbaric practices endured by enslaved Africans, calling for Britain to sever its ties with the abhorrent slave trade. His closing remarks, delivered with unwavering conviction, would resonate for years to come.

> *Having heard all of this you may choose to look the other way, but you can never say again, that you did not know.*

The House of Commons rejected the bill to end slavery, a terrible blow for abolitionists, Wilberforce refused to be deterred. He tirelessly campaigned in Parliament, year after year, chipping away at the opposition's resolve and continued to lead the cause of abolition until the passage of the slave trade ended.

In 1789, Josiah Wedgwood, a passionate abolitionist, designed a compelling symbol for the anti-slavery movement. It depicted a kneeling African man in chains, his plea etched in the inscription: "Am I not a man and a brother?" This evocative image resonated deeply, becoming a rallying point for abolitionists around the world.

A dominant voice joined the abolitionist cause, William Cowper, one of England's most prominent poets and hymn writers, deeply moved by the plight of enslaved Africans wrote several poems designed to ignite public outrage, notably, "The Negro's Complaint" offered a searing glimpse into the horrors of slavery, aiming to raise awareness of the human cost borne by the millions forcibly displaced across the globe.

John Newton, a former slave ship captain embodied a remarkable transformation, he was deeply burdened by his participation in the brutal trade. Profound remorse powered his conversion, Newton wrote in a pamphlet of his regret called, "Thoughts upon the Slave Trade."

> *"It will always be a subject of humiliating reflection to me, that I was once an instrument in a business at which my heart now shudders".*

He forged an unlikely alliance with the renowned poet William Cowper, together they produced an outstanding volume of hymns in 1779, a collection that included the now-iconic "Amazing Grace". This hymn, once a testament to a personal redemption, evolved into an evocative anthem for the abolitionist movement.

From the shadows of a brutal past powerful voices emerged in London. A dozen former enslaved men including Olaudah Equiano formed "The Sons of Africa.". United by a shared history of suffering, they worked relentlessly championing for the eradication of slavery. Their first hand accounts penned in works like Equiano's rousing autobiography, exposing the horrific realities of slavery in British colonies.

Olaudah Equiano

Portrait Painted by Allan Ramsay

Equiano's book became an instant sensation, a bestseller that transcended borders, published in England, America, Russia, Holland, and Germany. Alongside fellow author Ottobah Cugoano, whose book tells of the evil of slavery and Christian principles, both men served as a potent weapon for abolitionists. Traveling throughout England, they sold their books and delivered firsthand testimonies, igniting public outrage against the barbarity of the Atlantic slave trade.

Part 8

John's Contribution to the Cause

John began to use his position among the upper classes emerging as an appealing advocate against slavery. His articulate arguments delivered with a composed demeanour that belied his fiery passion, often eclipsing even the most seasoned abolitionists. However, his outspoken views clashed violently with the interests of the ruling class, many of whom profited handsomely from their West Indies plantations and enslaved labour.

John is noted in England at the time for: "His power of conversation" But his outspoken remarks were soon branded as "antics" by his critics; he would not be tolerated in England, reports of his "activism" reached the Prince of Wales. A mere two weeks after George had captivated the British monarchs, the stark contrast between the celebration of George's talent and the threat John now posed could not have been more evident.

The Prince of Wales made a move that would forever alter the course of John's life. He claimed that because of John's drinking, gambling and sheer brutality towards his own son, ultimately forced George to run away and seek refuge with him at his palace. In spite of the fact it had been documented that George was already living at the Pavilion since August 1789 and was being sponsored by the prince.

It seems the prince had planned and invented this story to keep George in his Pavilion. He refused to relinquish him to his father. His letter is a contradiction of what he said happened.

In an official note by HRH the prince of Wales

> "After years of hearing about the talents of George Bridgetower, I have finally taken him into my Patronage, he will live in my Royal Pavilion in Brighton teaching me music theory and playing in my personal band, this will mean taking the boy away from his parents, but I'm sure he will understand the benefits of this; after all, who would turn down the fame and fortune of being the Prince Regent's favourite? I will pay the father £25.00 and take care of his son".
>
> Signed, the Prince regent

John, heartbroken and totally powerless, was given permission to visit George occasionally. Just until the prince seized full guardianship of George.

At the age of eleven. George's future was no longer his own. He was swept into the prince's orbit, destined to become his personal musician for the royal court's entertainment at the newly built Brighton Pavilion.

This newspaper article was published on the 14th August 1789, and reappeared two months later.

Newspaper 14 October 1789 Chester Chronicle

"The musical world is likely to be enriched by the greatest phenomenon ever heard... A youth of 10 years old, a pupil of the immortal Haydn, he performs the most difficult pieces on the violin and goes through all the mazes of sound with wonderful spirit, execution and delicacy. His name is George Bridgetower a stable plant of African growth. Thus, do we find that genius does not solely belong to the tincture of the skin. He is now at Brighton Pavilion, under the patronage of the prince of Wales".

The prince's actions shattered John's dreams. He had envisioned his son flourishing as a free man, navigating a world increasingly critical of slavery. Now, that future was in tatters. George, no longer John's son but the prince's prize possession, confined within a gilded cage, the Brighton Pavilion.

His musical talents were no longer a source of pride, but a tool to be wielded at the prince's whim, a constant reminder of the freedom he'd been denied.

The prince, however did invest in George, he handpicked his tutors, meticulously curating his education and as his favourite musician, George revelled in a life of luxury. He forged bonds with fellow artists, basking in the prince's patronage. George, unlike his outspoken father possessed a quiet, melancholic demeanour at just eleven years old a shadow of loss hung over him, would he ever see his mother and brother again.

For the next six months, his father strutted around England burning with a righteous fury, like a mighty African emperor. His presence, a very public rebuke, dressed in exotic Eastern attire, he became a walking symbol of defiance. He frequented his son's concerts, his booming voice, a constant reminder of a stolen future.

John's passion for abolition was fuelled by rage and fuelled by his knowledge of injustice. The ruling class, once indifferent, now found themselves agitated by his eloquent pronouncements and unwavering resolve.

Then came the Pantheon Masquerade Ball, a glittering spectacle attended by the Prince of Wales himself, alongside the Dukes of York and Clarence. John's arrival shattered the night's light heartedness. He was not there to play by their rules, dressed not in finery but in the coarse garb of a slave, John stood as a living indictment of the very institution they upheld.

The masquerade, meant for amusement for the privileged, had morphed into a stage for his audacious defiance. Their enjoyment curdled into a cold fury, they understood the message painted by John, sickened by his antics they retaliated.

Newspapers were their well oiled machines of influence. They poised to strike back with a barrage of carefully crafted slander. Soon the newspapers were filled with venomous attacks, designed to dismantle John's reputation and silence his voice.

A Series of Newspaper Articles were Published

January 1790 Chronicle

John Bridgetower was obnoxious to the Genteel English public after having appeared At a function of the Prince of Wales, advocating the abolition of slavery.

February 13-16 Chronicle 1790

The African Prince, as he is styled, appeared as an advocate for the abolition of slavery, his character something of a Mungo stump.

The narrative John had meticulously cultivated, praised for his "fascinating manner and taste in dress," lay in tatters. A smear campaign encouraged by the prince painted stories of drunken escapades, dishonesty, and a callous act of gambling away his son for personal gain. These fabricated stories were adopted by researchers and became the accepted truth.

A violent scene at the performance of the Messiah in Covent Garden, caused by the African Prince.

11th March 1790, The General Evening Post

'The African Prince, who insisted, in the most insolent manner, that the chorus be repeated, throwing the audience and band into confusion. "Turn him out" was the general cry and after a violent struggle, the African Prince was thrown out'

7th April 1790 Derby Mercury

'He styles himself an African Prince, upon what authority? We will not pretend to say, he is at present resident in a receptacle for lunatics and the Prince of Wales, with his wonted goodness, has humanely, taken the son under his Royal protection.

The relentless pursuit of justice earned John a new label: lunatic, he was confined within the walls of Bridewell, a notorious asylum for the deranged. HRH the Prince of Wales had been victorious in taking the young violin prodgy from his father. Now he could take the credit for nurturing George's talent.

The prince's cruelty had no bounds. Under his tyrannical command, John was whisked away from the asylum and exiled from England altogether. Ordered to return to his family in Germany, a crushing distance separating him from his beloved son. Stepping onto French soil, John found himself in a nation utterly transformed, revolution had swept across the land, toppling the French monarchy, the air was filled with a new energy, liberty, equality and even the abolition of slavery.

These heady ideals, championed by the Jacobin faction under the leadership of Maximilien Robespierre resonated deeply with John. News of this rebellion had ignited a blaze in French colonies, with millions of enslaved people rising in a desperate fight for freedom, Saint-Domingue, also known as Haiti, stood at the epicentre of this struggle.

John couldn't contemplate returning to Germany without his son. Three decades had passed by since Tacky's rebellion in Jamaica that had consumed his world, ripping him from his own mother and father. Now, a different fire burned propelling him back towards the West Indies. His destination was not Jamaica but the volatile French colony of Haiti, a choice shrouded in the complexities of his own past.

The Civil Rights Document

The Declaration of the Rights of Man had been set by the National Constituent Assembly of France.

Part 9

Haiti 1791

Dutty Boukman, was enslaved in Jamaica, his fearsome temper and defiance was unwavering, resulting in him being sold to a French plantation owner in Haiti. There his leadership grew, becoming a Voodoo priest, he stood alongside Mambo Cécile Fatima. They orchestrated ceremonies, with inspiring words of freedom, to slaves dehumanised by French landowners. A rebellion soon roared to life in northern Haiti, with some two thousand following his lead.

Dutty Boukman

Imaginary vision of Boukman

His leadership proved tragically short-lived. captured by the French in 1791, he faced a brutal execution. His head displayed as a gruesome warning to the rebels hoping this would extinguish the rebellion, however, the French underestimated the power of Dutty Boukman. His death served as a potent symbol of the revolution that would rage across the island.

Toussaint Louverture, a man forged in the throes of slavery, arose as a crucial figure in the Haitian fight for freedom. His journey from enslaved person to revolutionary general defied expectations. A brilliant strategist, he meticulously built a formidable army, his keen eye recognizing and recruiting skilled military minds, who would become the backbone of the Haitian resistance. Among his generals were notable figures like Moïse-Jacques Dessalines and Henri Christophe.

Toussaint Louverture

1743-1803

Another appointee was John Bridgetower, an unlikely candidate, he hadn't fought any battles. Yet, Louverture, acknowledging John's passion and intellect, appointed him as Lieutenant General Mentor. This unprecedented pairing promised a fascinating chapter in the Haitian Revolution. As the Haitians' fight for freedom burned on, the ideals of liberty and equality roared across the Atlantic.

Paris the heart of the French Revolution was ablaze. Maximilien Robespierre, a passionate advocate for liberty and equality, rose to power in France on 4th February 1794.

Maximilien Robespierre

1758-1794

One of his first acts was the abolishment of slavery throughout the French colonies, this momentous decision sent a powerful validation to the Haitian fight for freedom and the millions more toiling under the yoke of French landowners in other colonies who could now dare to dream of a future free from chains.

The National Convention:

> *Declares the abolition of negro slavery in all the colonies; consequence it decrees that all men, without distinction of colour, residing in the colonies are French citizens and will enjoy all the rights assured by the constitution.*

The Haitian independence was far from over, while the revolutionaries celebrated Robespierre's abolition of slavery, a new threat emerged. The British and Spanish, harbouring ambitions of their own, attempted to snatch control of the newly freed colony. In a turn of events, Haitian forces united with their former French oppressors and together they were victorious. Haiti, tasting a fragile freedom, remained loyal to France for a few more fleeting years.

Robespierre implemented a series of reforms aimed at levelling the social playing field. Wealthy citizens in France faced increased taxes, a measure designed to fund social programs and education for the impoverished. This redistribution of resources, whilst intending to uphold the revolutionary ideals inevitably sparked tensions with the very class that had previously held the reins of power.

Quote by Maximilien Robespierre

> *The secret of freedom*
> *lies in educating people,*
> *whereas the secret of tyranny is in*
> *keeping them ignorant.*

Robespierre's radical reforms, generated by his strong beliefs in equality, caused a divide. Whilst they struck a chord with the downtrodden, the wealthy were enraged by the increased taxes, even those within the revolutionary ranks. Anxieties grew concerning his increasingly centralised power and simmering tensions reached boiling point. Just five months after Robespierre took office at the Hôtel de Ville, a group of ninety opponents launched a daring coup, storming the building and capturing him. He was executed without trial, along with twenty-one of his associates, Robespierre's demise dealt a crushing blow to the millions he had just liberated from slavery in the French colonies.

Maximilien Robespierre's fight for liberty and equality, became a cautionary tale, his legacy remains a subject of fierce debate among historians, a testament to the complex and often bloody path of revolution.

The winds of change swept through France once more. Napoleon Bonaparte, a charismatic but ruthless leader, ascended to power in 1799. His vision for the French colonies stood in stark contrast to the ideals of the revolution. In a devastating betrayal of the principles of the Declaration of the Rights of Man. Napoleon set his sights on the reintroduction of slavery throughout the French empire.

This audacious decree shattered the fragile peace between Haiti and France. The dream of freedom was once again under threat.

Napoleon Bonaparte

1769-1821

The embers of war in Haiti were rekindled, Napoleon, blinded by ambition and greed, set his sights on reversing the revolution's legacy. General Leclerc, his brother-in-law, received secret orders: to seize control of Haiti and restore the institution of slavery; he was to leave no blacks above that of captain on the island; this decree was a hideous betrayal of the ideals that had once bound Haiti and France together.

Leclerc, at the helm of a formidable force, set sail for Haiti. "The Elite of the French Army," some fifteen thousand strong alongside a contingent of five thousand Polish soldiers. Poland, desperate to secure French support against their own invaders, had agreed to fight for their former oppressors, this unholy alliance catapulted by Napoleon's ruthless pragmatism, would soon clash with the unwavering Haitian resolve for freedom.

Accompanying Leclerc on the Haitian expedition was a high-ranking military officer, of mixed heritage, he was the result of an illicit affair between an English aristocrat and an African valet. Born in Poland and raised by his stepfather, Konstanty Jablonowski, a Polish colonel and nobleman, who wanted an heir to follow in his military footsteps.

Brigadier General Jablonowski

1769-1802

At fourteen, Wladyslaw Jablonowski was sent to the prestigious Académie de Brienne, fate placing him alongside a fellow student named Napoleon Bonaparte. Their paths diverged sharply from the outset; Bonaparte, consumed by a deep prejudice, treated Wladyslaw with utter contempt. This early encounter left an indelible mark on Wladyslaw, a potent reminder of the ugliness that lurked beneath the surface of even the most privileged circles. Despite this, Wladyslaw, distinguished himself on the battlefield, defending both

France and Poland with valour. Recognition from Bonaparte remained elusive. Finally, under pressure from the military. Napoleon assigned Wladyslaw to the Haitian campaign as a Brigadier General, leading a combined force of Polish and French troops to crush the independence movement led by Toussaint Louverture.

Given their shared aristocratic backgrounds in Poland, Wladyslaw Jablonowski and John Bridgetower likely moved in the same circles in Poland. Both undoubtedly fostered a sense of connection and loyalty to Poland, even though they found themselves on opposing sides of the Haitian conflict.

Beneath the surface of the French-Polish alliance an uneasiness festered, Polish soldiers felt the sting of inequality that stirred up simmering resentment. A growing bitterness beneath their forced unity, a potential fracture that could shatter the already fragile alliance.

As the battle raged, General Leclerc made a calculated move. He extended an olive branch inviting the Haitian generals to peace talks. Wary but desperate for an end to the bloodshed they arrived with a proposal to adhere to the National Convention's decree.

Haiti's sovereignty to remain under French rule and the Haitian people to be granted the same rights as their French counterparts.

However, the promise of peace was a sham. In a shocking act of treachery, Leclerc's forces seized the unsuspecting Haitian leaders. Bound in irons, they were shipped off to France, their dreams of freedom dashed in a single, brutal manoeuvre.

Leclerc's betrayal to the Haitian peace talks disturbed everyone on the island including the Polish generals. This resulted in hundreds of Polish soldiers deserting the French and joining forces with the Hatitans, the very people they were sent to subdue. The Polish soldiers who remained under French command became increasingly insubordinate, their movements sluggish, their hearts no longer in the fight.

Amid this uprising speculation swirled around the roles of General Bridgetower and Brigadier Jablonowski; had they influenced the Polish to defection? The possibility of their involvement adds another layer of intrigue to this complex conflict.

The fate of Brigadier General Jablonowski remains unclear. 'Allegedly', yellow fever claimed him soon after he had arrived on the island. But rumours of a more sinister end, 'execution' for treason to France linger?

With Toussaint Louverture imprisoned, the mantle of leadership fell upon Jean-Jacques Dessalines, a man hardened by the toils of revolution. Leclerc's gamble on quelling the revolution had backfired spectacularly. He had failed to grasp the unwavering determination of Toussaint's meticulously trained army, driven by a righteous anger at French betrayal. Talks were a thing of the past. The atrocities inflicted upon the Haitian people by French landowners ran deep.

Dessalines led the Haitian forces in a relentless fight for freedom. The once-mighty French army crumbled under the Haitian onslaught, eventually relinquishing control of the island.

The cost of this failed expedition was staggering, out of twenty thousand French and Polish soldiers who set sail for Haiti, a mere three thousand returned to France, the fate of the Polish soldiers, who remained loyal the France is unclear, given the scale of total loss, it's highly unlikely any significant number of Polish soldiers survived.

In a desperate attempt to salvage their failure, the French resorted to a flimsy justification for their defeat, peddling the myth of Haitian immunity to yellow fever, a disease that had ravaged their ranks. However, a 2015 study by Cambridge University debunked this fallacy. Their research, titled "Immunity to Yellow Fever in History and Historiography," conclusively proved that there was no basis for the theory of racial immunity to yellow fever. This unsubstantiated claim, unfortunately, continues to echo today.

Haiti's victory was bittersweet, whilst they had secured their own freedom the fight to end slavery across all other French colonies remained a distant dream. Robespierre's idealistic decree of abolishing slavery had been ruthlessly reversed. Napoleon had effectively used his power. The Reign of Terror in other French colonies continued for another forty-six years.

Homage was paid to the Polish military who had fought alongside the Haitians. They were granted land just outside the capital, named Cazale. An integrated Polish community is still evident today, a testament to the unlikely bonds forged in the fires of revolution. Euphoria swept through Haiti as they celebrated their independence. The first country in the world to declare an end to slavery. The plight of the Polish soldiers has largely been untold throughout history.

Haiti's hard-won freedom came at a long-lasting cost. France made unrealistic demands on Haiti to pay one hundred and fifty million francs, as protection from them returning, a cynical ploy to recuperate their losses. This exorbitant financial burden took one hundred and twenty years to repay, shackling the nation's economy for generations, serving as a bitter reminder that the true cost of freedom can be measured not just in blood, but in crippling financial burdens.

The West's response to Haiti's victory added insult to injury. Portraying voodoo, as barbaric, the religion of a significant portion of Haitians. Fabricated drawings of savagery Haitian violence flooded western media. This convenient narrative deliberately ignored the atrocities the Haitians had endured during slavery.

To safeguard the colonial power structure, the West intentionally downplayed the complexities of Haiti's revolution. This manipulation of the narrative invited a punitive response. Western nations retaliated with crippling economic embargoes, a suffocating boycott that choked off Haiti's ability to import and export goods. The once wealthy nation was plunged into a devastating cycle of poverty, the lack of access to essential goods and resources from basic tools to raw materials. hampered the development of infrastructure, schools, hospitals, food and energy, the very foundations of a thriving society. The deliberate act of economic isolation reduced Haiti to one of the poorest countries in the world.

Haiti's Flag
Unity Creates Strength

Designed by Catherine Flon 1803

Haiti, a nation forever marked by the fight for freedom, still remains an elusive dream as they carry the weight of dictatorship, instability and natural disasters.

Part 10

Secret Decree

Haiti's victory against a European superpower sent shockwaves rippling across the Western world. Their triumph stood as a potent symbol of defiance, a beacon of hope for the enslaved and a terrifying challenge to the established order.

Napoleon's strategy of limiting black advancement in the military had a chilling effect that went way beyond the armed forces. It became a blueprint for a broader social effort to suppress the achievements and contributions of all people of African heritage.

Black excellence, heroism and intellectual prowess were deliberately downplayed or erased from history. This systematic silencing aimed to maintain a false narrative of black inferiority.

Those who had already achieved success or who possessed the potential for future greatness, found themselves deliberately excluded from narratives of progress and heroism. Their accomplishments were restrained, their contributions minimised and their stories relegated to the shadows. Such as:

Chevalier de Saint-Georges, a man once respected by all of France, died a couple of years prior to Haiti's independence. His contributions to classical music that had once captivated audiences across France, was disregarded, much of his work was destroyed, stolen, or hidden away as if he had never existed.

Benjamin Banneker, an American polymath, author, mathematician and astronomer, passed away in 1806. In a suspicious turn of events his house and laboratory caught fire on the very day of his funeral, destroying the vast majority of his life's work.

 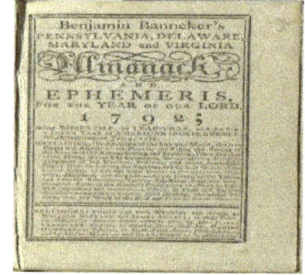

Generals such as Thomas Alexandre Dumas, were stripped of their ranks. His son, Alexandre Dumas, one of the most legendary French writers of his time whose novels included 'The Three Musketeers' and 'The Count of Monte Cristo'. His African heritage was completely disregarded as were the black heroes in his books and poems.

American inventor, engineer and poet, Lewis Howard Latimer, wasn't just a bright mind he was instrumental in illuminating the world. His groundbreaking contribution to the electric lightbulb, called the long-lasting carbon filament, was the key that unlocked the potential for electric lighting.

Jan Ernst Matzeliger's invention, the shoe-lasting machine, revolutionised the footwear industry. With a single stroke, daily production skyrocketed from fifty pairs to an astonishing seven hundred. This innovation slashed shoe prices worldwide, making comfortable footwear accessible to the masses for the first time.

Matthew Henson, was an African American explorer, who accompanied Robert Peary on seven Arctic voyages for nearly two decades, whilst Peary was hailed as a hero Henson was erased from the narrative.

Left in the Shadows

Granville T. Woods, a prolific American inventor, patented the Synchronous Multiplex Telegraph in 1887. This innovation sparked a legal battle with Thomas Edison, who contested its originality. Despite a costly lawsuit, Woods emerged victorious, securing his rightful credit for the invention. However, even this win couldn't erase the unfair dismissal of his brilliance. Wood's significant contributions went unrecognised.

Walter Tull was an English professional footballer and British Army officer in the First World War, he died for his country. Just like thousands of other soldiers of African heritage, who made the ultimate sacrifice for their country only to be overlooked.

Phillis Wheatly was born in Africa and enslaved aged seven in America, where she was noted for her intellect. Her book of poetry was published in 1773 in London. Her legacy has been largely forgotten.

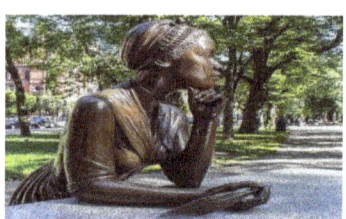

This strategy to exclude people of African heritage from platforms that allowed them to be admired by a wider world continued well into the 20th century.

The Sensational 1969 Summer of Soul

This cultural celebration was disregarded and shelved for fifty years. It promoted ingenuity, admiration and black pride.

Part 11
John Polgreen Bridgetower
1754-1817

Betrayed and broken, the Haitian generals, who were taken to France, found themselves cruelly imprisoned. Toussaint Louverture, the very soul of the revolution, perished in April 1803, he starved to death within the confines of a freezing fortress. Lieutenant General Mentor Bridgetower, however, faced a different fate. Possibly, due to his prominant connections he was separated from his comrades and shipped back to England. Upon reaching England Bridgetower was once again incarcerated within the walls of Bridewell Asylum.

Bridewell Asylum London

Coincidentally at this time his son, George, who had been a member of the Prince of Wales's personal orchestra for fourteen years, was promptly granted leave to visit his mother and brother in Germany.

Curiously, upon George's departure arrangements were discreetly made for annual payments to be sent to his mother in Germany from the British royal staff accounts.

The British press reported in 1805 on John's confinement in Bridewell Asylum, shrouding the reason for his incarceration in secrecy. Their articles cast doubt on John's credibility with a condescending tone.

The English Provincial Newspaper 1805

The pretender, John Polgreen Bridgetower otherwise Lieutenant General Mentor, lately serving under Toussaint Louverture, otherwise the Black Prince. This person speaks fluent English, French, German, Italian, and Polish, a man of 'colour', a fine figure about 40 years of age, is in confinement'.

Maria Bridgetower died in Germany in 1807. Payments from the Prince of Wales's royal staff accounts continued to be paid to her for another ten years after her death. These payments ceased in 1817, the year John took his last breath at the age of sixty-three. He had been in confinement for fifteen years.

The money paid by HRH was never claimed by Maria nor her sons, even after notices were placed in German and British newspapers, years later.

Whilst we have illuminated parts of John's extraordinary journey, much remains shrouded in mystery, His death in 1817 was recorded under the poor laws at St Martins in the Field London.

The Prince of Wales

The prince selfishly married Maria Fitzherbert, a catholic woman, in a secret ceremony, British law forbade catholics from becoming British monarchs, hence the marriage was not recognized.

The prince's extravagant lifestyle continued to rack up debt. To remedy this the King offered to pay his debts, on the condition he married his cousin, Caroline of Brunswick. A loveless marriage took place and as soon as their daughter, princess Charlotte, was born the prince expelled his wife Caroline from the palace. Ostracised and unwanted, she eventually fled to Germany.

Princess Charlotte was the Prince Regent's only legitimate heir; when she grew up she married Prince Leopold of Saxe-Coburg. Their union was seen by the nation as a cornerstone of national stability within the British royal family. Sadly, in 1817, during childbirth, complications claimed Princess Charlotte's life and that of her stillborn son. Britain was plunged into deep mourning.

The Prince of Wales ascended the throne in 1820. His coronation was the most lavish and expensive in British history. The ceremony was marred by the absence of Queen Caroline, his estranged wife; although she had returned to England, she was denied entry to Westminster Abbey, by order of the new King George 1V. Caroline suffered a public humiliation. Falling suspiciously ill that same night, she died two weeks later.

Prince of Wales courtier wrote in his diary

> *A more contemptible, cowardly selfish, unfeeling dog does not exist There have been good and wise kings but not many of them and this I believe to be one of the worse.*

King George IV embodied the twilight of the Hanoverian dynasty. He forever bore the weight of public scorn, his extravagant spending and scandalous affairs cast a long shadow over his reign. He retreated from the disapproving gaze of the nation, becoming a recluse within the walls of Windsor Castle. Upon his death in 1830, the crown passed down to his brother, Prince William IV. A seasoned sailor in his youth, he had spent years navigating the rough waters of the West Indies and North America.

Part 12

George Polgreen Bridgetower

Reuniting with his mother and brother Frederick, George found himself immersed in a thriving musical scene, Frederick, a gifted cellist by the age of twenty-one, had carved a niche for himself in German musical circles, his fluency in languages served a dual purpose: he offered his services as a 'West Indian English tutor' acknowledging the racial prejudice at the time.

Frederick, bursting with pride at George's association within Britain's royal musical circles, secured an introduction for him to meet Ludwig van Beethoven. A titan in the world of classical music, a man of intense passion. He harboured a well-known eccentricity in his personal habits, he also battled depression and moments of unpredictable behaviour. Beethoven was a hopeless romantic who yearned for love; he had proposed marriage several times to different women, each rejection leaving him more volatile.

Beethoven and George's friendship blossomed, inspired by a mutual appreciation for each other's work, Beethoven composed a new violin sonata specifically for George. The Vienna morning concert at the Augarten Pavilion was the stage for their historic debut. The performance was a resounding triumph and the audience erupted in applause in the electrifying aftermath.

Beethoven, perhaps carried away by the moment, proclaimed from the stage, "Once more, my dear fellow!" He further solidified their bond by presenting George with a tuning fork and initially dedicating the sonata to him, calling it the "Bridgetower Sonata."

Ludwig Van Beethoven

1770-1827

Their idyllic collaboration, however, was not destined to last. Beethoven, ever the passionate soul, took umbrage at a careless remark George made about a woman he was fond of at the time, enraged he snatched back the dedication. In George's place, he inscribed the name of another violinist, Rodolphe Kreutzer.

Ironically, Kreutzer was not an admirer of Beethoven's work and refused to play the sonata, as it was too difficult. Despite this the music itself thrived, forever, known as the Kreutzer Sonata.

Historical accounts often portray George as fading into obscurity after his disagreement with Beethoven. The truth is he was no longer given a platform to be seen by the western world as the prevailing attitude to disregard the accomplishments of people of African heritage had well and truly set in. This systemic bias effectively silenced his talent and relegated him to the margins of the classical music world.

George Polgreen Bridgetower

Although largely overlooked, George remained earnest within the musical circles of the time. He received significant accomplishment securing a permanent membership in the prestigious Philharmonic Society. His brother Frederick joined him in England and together they navigated a world that deliberately undermined their talent. Frederick found love and married Eliza Guy in 1808. Their union was blessed.

with two children: Catherine, a daughter and Frederick Jr. Just five years after their marriage Frederick Sr. passed away, leaving Eliza a young widow with two small children. Throughout the years George remained a pillar of support for Eliza and her children. He ensured they received a good education, young Frederick Jr. followed in his father's footsteps, eventually becoming a professor of music himself. Catherine married and raised a family. Notably, both Frederick's children carried the torch of their African heritage with pride, passing it down to future generations who continue to celebrate it even today.

National Archives Reference C 13/1915

George met a young woman, Mary Leach, in 1815 she was from Kensington, an affluent area of London, unlike her more conventional siblings, Mary chafed against societal constraints, in a startling act of defiance she once cut off all her hair, storing it in a heart-shaped box secured with a lock and key, this bold gesture hinted at a rebellious spirit and a desire for autonomy, Mary's inheritance, shared equally with her brother Edward, placed her in a position of financial security. As the sole male heir, Edward assumed responsibility for managing the family's wealth and business affairs, Clara, their half-sister from their mother's previous marriage, received a separate, small inheritance of five thousand pounds.

George was a resident of Highgate, a prosperous area of London. Despite their seventeen-year age difference, between them their connection blossomed and they married in March 1816 at St. George's Church, Hanover Square. Their union was soon blessed with the arrival of their daughter, Felicity, in November 1817. Mary's brother, Edward, harboured disapproval of her marriage to a man of colour, but his love for his niece eventually outweighed his reservations.

George's marriage to Mary involved him in the family business alongside Edward. Unlike Edward, George showed little enthusiasm for their business or wealth, possibly due to his years living in royal palaces or the fact he was a musician. This detachment led Edward, who preferred livelier company, to describe George as "gloomy and somewhat melancholy."

After three years of marriage. George and Mary were drawn to the charm of Italy. They relocated to Rome with their daughter. Once in Italy they quickly mastered the culture and seamlessly integrated into high society, their social circle soon expanded to include a captivating figure; the young and handsome Italian nobleman, Carlos Busca Visconti.

Carlos, a bachelor burdened with securing his family's lineage, felt the weight of responsibility to produce an heir, even more acutely since his only sibling, Antonio, stubbornly refused marriage.

A forbidden passion between Mary and Carlos led to a scandal in Rome. In 1824, Mary confessed the affair to George, shattering their marriage. George left for France, seeking solace in anonymity, while Felicity stayed with her mother.

Carlos Busca Visconti

1791-1850

In Italy, Mary, now known as Maria and Carlos threw caution to the wind, their affair blooming openly despite the disapproval of his aristocratic family. Their passionate defiance was briefly interrupted in 1826 by his scheming mother, she persuaded him to embark on a journey to Egypt hoping it would end their affair; Carlos was very much attracted to the world of Ancient Egypt. He spent some time in the south of Cairo, where one of the oldest pyramids in Africa is located called Saqqara. He returned to Rome at the year's end, not only with a mysterious trove of Egyptian treasures but with renewed passion for Mary. His family were outraged with the shame that she had brought upon their family, blaming her for Carlos's delay in marrying a suitable woman to carry on the family lineage.

In the chill of Christmas 1827, some three years after George had left, he returned to Italy, first to see his daughter Felicity and secondly, he carried legal papers for a formal separation from Mary. He stayed in Rome until spring, on returning to London he filed the signed documents with his solicitors on 12th May 1828. Six months later, he received word that Mary had given birth to a son, Lodovico Bridgetower.

A murmur snaked through Rome's social circles, Mary's unexpected pregnancy, perfectly timed with George's return. Mary and Carlos had been having an affair for years without issue, their genuine affection for each other soon extinguished the gossip, for over a decade, they defied the rigid social norms of the times.

Their affair was forever stilled; on 3rd July 1835, Mary died unexpectedly, suspected of food poisoning; leaving an unimaginable void. Felicity, now a young woman of eighteen and Lodovico, a bewildered child of seven, were left to grapple with the sudden absence of their mother, the once vibrant melody of their lives had been replaced by an unhappy silence.

Grief morphed into fury for Felicity. Her mother's death wasn't an ending, she publicly pointed a finger with an accusation of murder at the Busch Visconte family, their wealth and power a threatening shadow over her.

She made reports to the police and pronouncements to the press of the questionable circumstances surrounding her mother's passing. Felicity's voice, laced with conviction, claimed her mother's silencing was the only way to bury the affair between her mother and Carlos. The Busch family were the only ones powerful enough, the police made no investigation.

When her father, George, returned to Italy, Carlos came to him shrouded in a veil of mourning, he approached George with a proposition, asking if he could take young Lodovico and raise him as his own son, within the luxurious walls of the Visconti palace. George, burdened by his own complicated emotions, found himself in a difficult position, he barely knew the child,

The request from the man whose family Felicity suspected of murdering her mother, was a heavy load to bear, he had to do what was best for Lodovico, he knew Carlos loved the child and could give him more than he could ever dream of; George agreed with his request.

Felicity was distraught. How could her father so readily entrust her brother, his son to the very people she believed were responsible for their mother's death? His apparent indifference to Mary's passing and his willingness to hand Lodovico over shattered her. She furiously cried out *"I will never forgive him. He's the cruellest, most unfeeling person I know."* The strain on their relationship became so intense that Felicity left their home and moved in with her mother's friend Vittoria and her husband Louis Mazzara, who ran a boarding house.

George and Felicity's relationship had compleatly broken down; the weight of his daughter's hatred sat heavily on his shoulders. He made arrangements for Felicity's welfare and returned to France.

When Vittoria succumbed to illness, Felicity remained at the boarding house. An intense relarionship blossomed between her and Louis Mazzara, when she turned twenty-one their love story culminated in marriage. She was, also, now of age to claim her inheritance.

Felicity returned to England with her husband Louis. However, upon arrival, her dreams were dashed, her uncle Edward, was enraged by her marriage to a man he deemed "not a gentleman of property" by his own narrow standards, he slammed the door shut.

The information needed to access her rightful inheritance remained frustratingly out of her reach, Edward's disapproval a barrier between her and her future. Swallowing her pride, Felicity knew there was only one option, she had to reach out to her father, who was still in France. George, spurred by a renewed sense of purpose, returned to England and wasted no time. A court order against Edward landed with a thud, a legal challenge to his control. In the courtroom, Felicity pleaded with her uncle, not just for her inheritance, but for a heart-shaped casket her mother had left behind in the family home. It held the lock of her mothers hair, a "precious memory" she said in the court. The court ruled in her favour. Edward had to comply; he was forced to release her inheritance and to share the profits from their successful businesses.

Forgiving her father for surrendering Lodovico to Carlos remained a bitter pill for Felicity to swallow but a seed of understanding was planted, by her father who truly believed it was in the boy's best interest, with that seed, a fragile reconciliation bloomed between them.

With Louis by her side, Felicity returned to Italy, their love was solidified by the arrival of two sons, Felix and Nicholas. Visits from George, now a grandfather, were no longer fraught with tension, but filled with the joy of rediscovery, each visit became a cherished bridge across the miles, a testament to the hard-won peace they had finally forged, a balm to the wounds of the past. Felicity never gave up on seeking justice for her mother fifteen years after her mother's death she and Louis continued with her accusations of her mother's death.

Glasgow Chronicle 29 May 1851

Signor Mazzara, an ingenious man, married to an English lady, has been arrested for having constructed a kind of moveable barricade and fortified the approach to Porta del Popolo during the war, such at any rate, is his supposed offence, but in reality the enmity of the powerful family of Busca Visconti and the desire to hush up the romantic story of his wife's wrongs and to avoid the investigation of her mother, Mrs Bridgetower's murder may be considered as the real motive of his imprisonment.

Carlos did finally take a wife, however the much anticipated marriage remained childless. The Busch Visconti family were seemingly cursed by an empty cradle.

Though Lodovico Bridgetower was like a son to Carlos, thirteen long years passed before he legally adopted him. The Busca family never accepted Lodovico; to ensure Lodovico inheritance, Carlos had to include special provisions in his will, a testament to the ever-present tension within the family.

Newspaper Liverpool Albion 13 January 1851

> *Marquis Visconti of Milan, the nobleman to whom I allude as being just now deceased, certainly had been an intimate acquaintance of Mrs Bridgetower and after her death, took so warm an interest in her little boy, that he took him to his palace, adopted him as his son, brought him up as a Marchesini, and has finally left him heir to the bulk of his immense property, to the great disgust, no doubt of his Milanese relations.*

Lodovico became the main beneficiary of Busca Visconti's affluent dynasty. He found solace in marriage to Clementina Lazarich, together, they built a life filled with joy, welcoming five daughters into the world, but tragedy struck a cruel blow, his wife died during the birth of their sixth child, leaving him a shattered widower, consumed by grief and unable to bear the gaping hole in his life, Lodovico ended his own life.

George nearing eighty years old, sought solace in a quaint cottage in Peckham London, frailty beckoned, prompting him to focus on one final act, to divide his estate while he still possessed the strength and also ensuring his brother-in- law, Edward was sharing the profits from the family businesses Mary and Edward had equally inherited.

An element of suspicion lingered within him, in 1854 a bill of complaint, a formal accusation of wrongdoing, written by George landed on the desk of Mr. Appleby, his solicitor in London. He named Felicity, her husband Louis and his grandsons, Felix and Nicholas, as plaintiffs in the chancery suit.

Edward, as it turned out he had been stealing money from the estate that was meant for Felicity and her family. After a gruelling legal battle, the court stripped Edward of his trustee duties.

George Polgreen Bridgetower took his last breath on the 29th February 1860. He bequeathed the rest of his estate to his wife's half-sister Clara, with whom he had remained close. George was laid to rest in a tomb, the echoes of his life fading into the cemetery's hushed embrace in Kensal Green London.

George Bridgetower's Tomb in London

After his death his family, driven by a profound yearning to reconnect with their lost African heritage. His grandsons and their cousins, the grandchildren of his brother Frederick, embarked on a daring quest to Abyssinia, the legendary homeland of their ancestors. They sought to uncover and understand their roots. In doing so, they unveiled the truth about the stolen Abyssinian Prince, filling them with pride in their ancient royal lineage.

They returned to England in 1867 and sought an audience with Lord Stanley, the British Foreign Secretary. They presented him with irrefutable proof of their ancestry, upon hearing their story he not only reported it to the British press, but also assured them that:

1867 Evening Post

England will not interfere with the Abyssinian succession.

And we suppose Sir Bridgetower vents his wrath against perfidious England.

Despite Lord Stanley's condescending dismissal of their evidence, the Bridgetower family refused to let their story be buried. His arrogance cast a long shadow, threatening to obscure their truth. Yet, the legacy of the stolen Abyssinian Prince burned brightly in John Polgreen Bridgetower, the prince's son. Rising from the shackles of slavery with dignity and knowledge of his birthright, he became the custodian of their story. Driven by fierce determination, he ensured their truth would forever defy oblivion.

Epilogue

On the 25th of March 1807, British Parliament outlawed the Atlantic slave trade. It meant no more people would be taken from the African continent to join the three million they had already enslaved in British colonies.

However, the abhorrent practice of slavery continued within the British colonies. To compensate for the loss of imported labour, a brutal tactic emerged: the forced procreation of enslaved people. The violation of women and girls to produce a new generation of slaves increased tenfold.

Twenty-six years later in 1833 British Parliament finally eradicated slavery. However, a deeply unsettling chapter remained, as the government chose to compensate the forty-six thousand wealthy slave owners for their "losses," a staggering sum that burdened taxpayers for one hundred and eighty-two years.

The abolition of the Atlantic slave trade didn't signal an end to exploitation in Africa. European ships continued their relentless plunder, swapping human cargo for the continent's riches: gold, diamonds, platinum. Africa's wildlife became trophies for fleeting enjoyment, this is a practice that continues to plague the continent today.

The intense exploration today is for the estimated one hundred and twenty billion barrels of oil buried beneath the Okavango Delta in Botswana. This insatiable thirst for resources threatens to push wildlife to the brink of extinction. Bulldozers carve through the landscape, making way for oil rigs that pierce the earth's crust, polluting rivers and altering the climate forever.

The legacy of resource extraction continues. Sub-Saharan Africa grapples with over 100 mining operations across 37 countries. 59 companies are British, incorporated within the UK, with others nestled in British tax havens like Guernsey and Jersey.

Africa's Okavango Delta the devastation of oil spillages

Our planet's tapestry of life hangs in the balance. Protecting its biodiversity isn't a mere duty, it's a call for action. The time for deliberation has passed. We must unite, a global chorus of voices, to weave a sustainable future for ourselves and generations to come. Let's rise to the challenge and turn the tide before it's too late.

Twenty First Century Slavery

The shadow of slavery continues to darken the twenty first century, manifesting in bonded labour, forced labour, child exploitation, human trafficking. This persistent injustice demands constant vigilance.

Eradicating these forms of slavery requires global cooperation. The burden of compensation payments to former slave owners, technically impeded the British government's full participation in anti- slavery efforts.

This historical entanglement was finally severed in 2015, after one hundred eighty two years paving the way for England to introduce A Modern Slavery Act in 2015. It is today designed to combat slavery in the United Kingdom.

This act has set a global standard for combating human trafficking and exploitation, marking a step forward in the ongoing fight for justice.

We honour the memory of the millions whose lives were stolen, bodies exploited, and spirits crushed. We also remember those who fought and died for their freedom. Today, we stand in solidarity with those who continue to fight for freedom and equality.

www.ingramcontent.com/pod-product-compliance
Lightning Source LLC
Chambersburg PA
CBHW041303240426
43661CB00011B/1005